GARDEN GUIDES

THE COTTAGE GARDEN

SIENA

GARDEN GUIDES

THE COTTAGE GARDEN

POLLY BOLTON

Illustrations by
ELAINE FRANKS

A Siena book.
Siena is an imprint of Parragon Books.

This edition first published in 1996 by
Parragon Book Service Ltd
Unit 13–17, Avonbridge Trading Estate
Atlantic Road
Avonmouth
Bristol BS11 9QD

Produced by
Robert Ditchfield Ltd
Combe Court
Kerry's Gate
Hereford HR2 0AH

Text and artwork copyright © Parragon Book Service Ltd 1996
Photographs copyright © Robert Ditchfield Ltd 1996
This edition copyright © Parragon Book Service Ltd 1996

ISBN 0 75251 594 2

A copy of the British Library Cataloguing in Publication Data is
available from the Library.

Typeset by Action Typesetting Ltd, Gloucester
Colour origination by Mandarin Offset Ltd, Hong Kong
Printed and bound in Italy

ACKNOWLEDGEMENTS
Many of the photographs were taken in the author's nursery and garden, Nordybank Nurseries, Clee St.
Margaret, Craven Arms. The publishers would also like to thank the many people and organizations who have
allowed photographs to be taken for this book, including the following:

Mrs Anthony Anderson; Lucinda Aldrich-Blake; Barnsley House; Bromesberrow Place; Burford House, Tenbury
Wells; Lallie Cox, Woodpeckers, Marlcliff, Bidford-on-Avon; Richard Edwards, Well Cottage, Blakemere; Field
House, Clee St. Margaret; Frampton Manor; Lance Hattatt, Arrow Cottage, Weobley; Mr and Mrs James
Hepworth, Elton Hall; Hergest Croft Gardens; Mr and Mrs B. Howe; Kim Hurst, The Cottage Herbery, Mill
House, Boraston Ford; Mrs David Lewis, Ash Farm, Much Birch; Mottisfont Rose Gardens (National Trust); Mrs
R. Paice, Bourton House; Pentwyn Cottage Garden, Bacton; The Picton Garden, Colwall; Powis Castle (National
Trust); Royal Botanic Gardens, Kew; RHS Garden, Wisley; Malcolm Skinner, Eastgrove Cottage Gardens,
Shrawley; Snowshill (National Trust); Stone House Cottage, Kidderminster; Raymond Treasure, Stockton Bury
Farm, Kimbolton; Mrs Trevor-Jones, Preen Manor; David Wheeler, The Neuadd; Mrs Geoffrey Williams, Close
Farm, Crockham Hill; Woodlands, Bridstow.

CONTENTS

Poisonous Plants

In recent years, concern has been voiced about poisonous plants or plants which can cause allergic reactions if touched. The fact is that many plants are poisonous, some in a particular part, others in all their parts. For the sake of safety, it is always, without exception, essential to assume that no part of a plant should be eaten unless it is known, without any doubt whatsoever, that the plant or its part is edible and that it cannot provoke an allergic reaction in the individual person who samples it. It must also be remembered that some plants can cause severe dermatitis, blistering or an allergic reaction if touched, in some individuals and not in others. It is the responsibility of the individual to take all the above into account.

Water in the Garden

All water gardens are beautiful, but sadly they can be dangerous, mostly to children who can drown in even a few inches of water, or sometimes to adults. We would urge readers where necessary to take account of this and provide a reliable means of protection if they include water in the garden.

How to Use This Book

Where appropriate, approximate measurements of a plant's height have been given, and also the spread where this is significant, in both metric and imperial measures. The height is the first measurement, as for example 1.2m × 60cm/4 × 2ft. However, both height and spread vary so greatly from garden to garden since they depend on soil, climate and position, that these measurements are offered as guides only. This is especially true of trees and shrubs where ultimate growth can be unpredictable.

The following symbols are also used throughout the book:

◯ = thrives best or only in full sun
◐ = thrives best or only in part-shade
● = succeeds in full shade
E = evergreen

Where no sun symbol and no reference to sun or shade is made in the text, it can be assumed that the plant tolerates sun or light shade.

Plant Names

For ease of reference this book gives the botanical name under which a plant is most widely listed for the gardener. These names are sometimes changed and in such cases the new name has been included. Common names are given wherever they are in frequent use.

THE COTTAGE GARDEN

(*Above*) A close planting of forget-me-nots, pansies and the blue *Centaurea montana*.
(*Right*) Quintessential cottage borders with pinks, roses and foxgloves overhanging the path.

THE COTTAGE GARDEN is traditionally a small, densely planted plot, best described as delightful chaotic profusion. It is not too contrived and yet carefully tended, every available niche and space being used. Most of the garden will consist of paths and borders with small patches of grass near the house or beneath fruit trees. The dense borders which are the main characteristic of the cottage garden are planted with tall perennials, shrubs and ground-cover plants, interspersed with self-seeding annuals and biennials. Many of the plants have domestic uses as herbs, fruit, aromatics and bee-nectar plants. Salad plants and vegetables grow in small plots amongst the flowers or in vegetable plots surrounded by borders of herbs and aromatic plants, which deter insect pests from finding their 'host' vegetables.

The true cottage garden was not contrived and most of its space was devoted to food production. Flowers were tucked here and there and arrived through friends or were started from bits taken from the borders of the 'Big House'. Seeds came on boots, by birds and on the wind or were transplanted from hedgerow and meadow. Native plants which had abnormalities such as variegated leaves or white or double flowers were collected in such gardens since early times. Dotted planting, where plants of different characteristics are grown together, is a true feature of cottage gardens. Nowadays a sense of structure can be introduced by a clipped hedge, stone ornament, arch or seat.

HISTORY OF THE COTTAGE GARDEN

There is little written about cottage gardens prior to 1750. A cottager may have been any-

8

(*Left*) This painting, which dates from the end of the nineteenth century, is by Helen Allingham. Though realistic (note the washing on the line and the ramshackle fence), it exemplifies the ideal cottage in the country, old, pretty, its garden filled with plants.

(*Right*) A dreamy close planting of day-lilies and *Campanula lactiflora*.

one who worked on a big estate but did not live in the 'Big House', including farm workers, gardeners and dairymen or they may have been small farmers or country craftsmen. The medieval cottage garden was probably just a yard with animals, separated into sections by hurdles. One of the sections would be used for growing vegetables and corn, and the sections rotated each year. Farmstead gardens consisted of a small orchard, a turf area and rectangular beds for herbs and vegetables. These yeoman-farmer gardens became the inspiration for the grander small country houses which began to adopt the cottage gar-

den style by the late eighteenth century. Romantic cottage gardens also had features reminiscent of the pleasure gardens of medieval and Tudor manor houses such as topiary, arches, bowers and decorative trelliswork.

By the beginning of the twentieth century, the cottage garden had declined due to an increase in short-term tenancies of cottages and an increase in the urban population. The cottage garden style continued to evolve in the grander country cottages inhabited by relatively wealthy people. Garden writers such as William Robinson and Gertrude Jekyll in the

late nineteenth century, popularized the more informal and natural approach to gardening. In the 1970s the cottage garden style enjoyed another revival as part of the interest in wildlife and organic gardening. This interest is still gathering momentum.

DESIGN AND PLANNING

Few of us start a garden from scratch but inherit other peoples' mistakes and tastes in gardening. When starting, it is advisable to eradicate fiddly elements such as rockeries and weed-filled walls rather than spend valuable time trying to make them look pleasant.

Features like walls and paths were purely functional in old cottage gardens. Use any existing trees and shrubs, providing they do not obscure your best view nor have been planted too close to the house. A bit of shade in the garden can be useful, providing another kind of habitat for herbaceous plants. Decide where your paths, borders and grass areas will be and whether you need to break the garden into sections or 'rooms' by using trellises, fences and hedges. You may find that your soil varies in different areas of the garden: a dry well-drained patch is ideal for most herbs; a damp area can be transformed into a lush bog garden; and an area of subsoil and rubble can be dug out and made into a feature such as a sunken stone garden or a pond.

Before planting borders, as many weeds as possible should be removed, especially where perennials will be planted. Rotovating is not a good idea for a perennial bed since it chops up weed roots and multiplies them. (In a vegetable patch which is regularly cultivated, the rotovator has its uses.) The borders are now ready to be planted with shrubs, roses, and clumps of perennials.

Well-meaning friends will soon offer you pieces of herbaceous plants. If you see any sign of a perennial weed growing in the clump, throw the whole lot away. It is virtually impossible to completely remove weeds such as ground elder (*Aegopodium podagraria*) once they have grown into another plant. Scatter as many annual seeds as possible amongst your perennials. These will provide you with a show of dense colour for the first year and many will provide a seed bank of self-sown plants for future growing seasons.

Typical cottage plants, lupins and *Rosa* 'Albertine'.

MANAGEMENT

A friend who has been a cottage gardener for fifty years once told me that one must be prepared to 'waltz plants around the garden'. The random and informal style of cottage gardening results in some being planted in the wrong place. But many chance and happy unplanned plant associations will be discovered. Growing old-fashioned varieties of plants rather than modern hybrids will result in colour tones that tend to harmonize with each other. Making notes of plants that look good next to each other whilst visiting other gardens or looking through books will add to your repertoire of pleasing plantings.

Some gardeners rush to dead-head a plant once its flower is over but seed heads can be very attractive and provide food for seed-eating birds. The advantages of leaving perennial plants uncut through the winter are that the plants are better protected from cold and are not tempted to make growth during a warm spell and they will more readily seed down. They also provide food for birds and over-wintering sites for beneficial insects. Nutrients from the border plants are recycled, which helps maintain soil fertility. Borders can be cut back in early spring and carefully and selectively weeded. Mulching with a light covering of bark, lawn-mowings or leaf mould throughout the growing season, should result in less weeding the following spring. Each year note the plants that are becoming too large or rampant and move them to another site later in the season. The advantage of dense planting which is so characteristic of cottage gardens is that many plants will support each other and the need for staking will be reduced.

Nepeta, white foxgloves and geraniums form twin borders either side of the path which leads to an open door, encouraging you to walk beyond it.

THE COTTAGE GARDEN TODAY

The revival of interest in the cottage garden corresponds with the awareness of organic cultivation and the value of wildlife gardening. Many insect pests have natural insect predators and a wide range of plants, including wild flowers, in the garden helps to provide nectar and pollen needed at various stages of the predatory insect's life cycle. Trees and shrubs and carefully sited nest-boxes soon attract a variety of birds. The relatively undisturbed habitat of the mixed shrub and perennial border is an ideal habitat for hedgehogs. A small pond will soon be buzzing with aquatic life. Wildlife in the garden makes it a more rewarding place and reduces the need for chemical control of pests. Many wild flowers can be grown in borders where they may compete for beauty with garden varieties.

An interest in permaculture in the last few years is reflected in the revival of the cottage garden style of gardening. Every available niche is used to grow perennial plants. For example, a clematis will quite happily twine through a wall-rose or over a border shrub. This form of growing is ideal for a small garden where a much greater number and variety of plants can be grown. This ebullient profuse style copies nature so is not recommended for the tidy-minded gardener! Nature is often beautiful but rarely tidy. Colour, scent, texture together with serenity, birdsong and beauty will be yours in a cottage garden.

1. FRAMING AND FORMING

All gardens need their lines and boundaries drawn and this is true of even the abundantly planted cottage garden.

WALLS

THE SPECIALIZED HABITAT OF THE WALL has long been used by the cottager where ground space was limited. The sharp drainage of walls makes them ideal for alpine plants which will seed down readily and require little attention. Damp walls quickly become colonized by native ferns. Tall brick walls can be wired with vine eyes and planted with climbers or espalier fruit trees.

Grow scented shrubs to hang over walls, such as **roses** and **philadelphus** (mock orange). A good plant for the top of walls, shown below, is *Saxifraga* **'Aureopunctata'** (variegated London pride) with its leafy, mat-forming rosettes and pink flowers on thin stems. To its left is a **helianthemum** (rock rose), a spreading small shrub that flowers profusely in midsummer. In damper parts of walls, **ferns** will thrive, whilst plants such as the yellow *Corydalis lutea* (on the left) and purple **aubrieta** will seed into crevices.

STEPPING OUT

THE OLD CINDER PATHS AND STEPS of cottage gardens were purely functional, taking the shortest route to privvy or pigsty. When laying a path, playing around with curves which lead to focal points such as seats can make paths an interesting framework for the small garden.

Saxifraga moschata (**Mossy saxifrage**) A cushion plant, spreading over rocks and soil, which carries slender stems with terminal flowers in shades of red, pink or white. ◑, E, 20 × 45cm/ 8in × 1½ft

When making steps ensure the uprights are securely retained by stones or treated timber.

Place aromatic plants near a path to enjoy the fragrance which is released by touch. Herbs are excellent 'path-edgers'.

Old-fashioned pinks (dianthus) love to spread over dry surfaces without increasing from their root base. Trim after flowering.

Campanula poscharskyana Profusely-flowering plant, forming a low spreading clump. Early summer. 25 × 60cm/10in × 2ft

Erigeron karvinskianus Delicate daisy flowers are produced throughout the summer. Not fully hardy. ○, 15cm/6in × wide spread

◆ *This plant loves to freely seed on stone steps and in path crevices.*

The outline of this straight path is broken by attractive clumps of **Santolina neapolitana**. Santolinas, which are lovers of free-draining warm soils, produce masses of button flowers in summer. ○, E, 60 × 60cm/2 × 2ft

◆ *Santolinas are aromatic shrubs, hardy except in severe winters. Prune hard in late spring.*

MIXING MATERIALS IN PATHWAYS can be very effective; stone, gravel and slabs in matching tones when placed carefully provide a valuable foil for plants in adjoining borders. If in doubt keep to one material but this need not be a dull solution as brick and stone can be charmingly set.

STEPPING OUT

Thymes spread easily between stones of paths, withstanding some treading. Aromatic and colourful. ○, E, 10 × 60cm/4in × 2ft

Lysimachia nummularia (**Creeping Jenny**) Groundcover edging plant preferring moist soils. 15cm/6in × wide spread.

The outline of this path is made more interesting by planting of both tall and medium-height plants next to the path.

◆ *Dead-head plants next to gravel paths to avoid seeding.*

HEDGES

Clipped hedges and topiary have long been a feature of old cottage gardens. Almost any hedging shrub can be used for topiary. Picket fences and woven hazel hurdles provide attractive barriers and backdrops to newly planted hedges or borders. Hazel hurdles have been used for hundreds of years to separate areas of the garden and to protect from stock and wind.
A natural hedge of native trees and shrubs, clipped occasionally, provides a valuable habitat for wildlife.

***Viburnum opulus* (Guelder rose)** Large spreading shrub ideal for planting in a mixed hedge with wonderful autumn tints and red berries (poisonous). White flowers in umbels in late spring. 4m/13ft

Some hedges, such as *Lonicera nitida* and box may have to be wired when a straight edge is needed.

When planting a double hedge, stagger the two lines of planting to thicken the base.

***Taxus baccata* (Yew)** Traditionally used for clipping and topiary. All parts are poisonous. E, 12m/40ft

***Crataegus* (Hawthorn)** Small tree or can be clipped in a more formal hedge. White, pink or red flowers in early summer. 9m/30ft

***Ligustrum ovalifolium* 'Aureum'** Golden form of privet. Needs clipping two or three times a year. E or semi-E. 2.7m/9ft

***Buxus sempervirens* (Box)** Aromatic, glossy leaves. Slow-growing, ideal for a low hedge. E, 3m/10ft

***Rosa* 'Roseraie de l'Haÿ'** Vigorous shrub rose. Large attractive hips. Early summer to autumn. 2 × 2m/6 × 6ft

ON A DIFFERENT LEVEL, there are the low-growing relaxed plants that lend themselves to use at the front of beds or beside paths. Often sprawling but rarely unwelcome, they can be allowed to tumble at the feet of larger plants behind them. Some, like the pinks, can be also used to make an informal ribbon at the edge of small borders.

Dianthus **'Mrs Sinkins'** Double, deliciously clove-scented flowers. Also pink form. Summer. ○, E, 20 × 30cm/8in × 1ft

Geranium sanguineum **(Bloody cranesbill)** Flowers in early summer. Dead-head for repeat flowering. 25 × 30cm/10in × 1ft

Phuopsis stylosa Spreads into large clumps. Pale pink flowers in summer. Tolerates moist soil. 12.5 × 60cm/5in × 2ft

Stachys byzantina **(Lamb's ears)** Downy leaves with flowering spikes of pink/purple. Spreads to large clump. ○, 45 × 60cm/ 1½ × 2ft

Viola cornuta alba Spreads to dense tuft by rootstock. Flowers white, pale blue or mauve throughout summer. 7.5 × 60cm/3in × 2ft

Alchemilla mollis **(Lady's mantle)** Downy, rounded leaves. 45 × 60cm/ 1½ × 2ft

◆ *Gather flowering spikes when fully opened to dry for winter decoration.*

QUIET TIMES

***Lonicera periclymenum*
'Graham Thomas'** Grow this honeysuckle into trees or on pergolas and walls. 6m/20ft

***Laburnum × watereri* 'Vossii'** Small tree with many long racemes of yellow flowers in early summer. All parts are poisonous. 6m/20ft

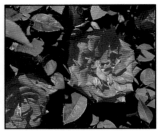

***Rosa* 'Zéphirine Drouhin'** Shrub rose which can be trained as a climber up to 4m/13ft. Early to late summer.

***Clematis viticella* 'Etoile Violette'** Vigorous climber with deep purple flowers 10cm/4in. in diameter throughout summer. Prune dead wood in spring. 6m/20ft

Position garden seats to provide pleasing views of the garden or vistas beyond.

Garden paths leading to seats and arbours are a timeless feature of old gardens and they should be positioned with care.

The best seats are simple ones. Anything grand, elaborate or too modern looks out of place.

Rambling roses with plenty of growth around their base often provide better subjects for arches than climbing roses which may be bare and straggly and are better suited to walls. Here the same variety rose has been planted on each side of a simple rustic arch.

◆ *Once-flowering roses may have clematis growing up with them to provide interest later in the summer.*

SEATS, TRELLISES, ARBOURS AND BOWERS were all features of cottage gardens, especially the grander romantic garden of the eighteenth and nineteenth century. Trellises are ideal for providing shelter, screens and vertical dimensions in flat gardens. Trellises and arches should harmonize in style and materials and provide support for a variety of plants grown in sun and shade. Climbers with pendant flowers are well-suited to bowers as it is possible to see into their blossom.

Lilium regale One of the most beautifully scented white lilies. Well-suited to growing in pots and placed by a seat. 1m/3ft

QUIET TIMES

A variety of climbing plants can be grown together. Careful pruning can prevent one plant dominating the growing space.

Scent overhead from climbers on a bower as well as to hand from potted plants is worth planning.

Aromatic plants such as rosemary (*Rosmarinus officinalis*), lavender (*Lavandula*) and southernwood (*Artemisia abrotanum*) provide fragrance next to garden seats. Treneague chamomile planted in crevices underfoot adds pineapple scent.

◆ *Crevice plants often need ample moisture in the soil to thrive and spread over stones.*

2. Roses and Climbers

A cottage garden could never be without roses and the climbing plants that adorn its walls and trees.

With their range of habits, foliage and flowers, old shrub roses are perfect for the informal style of cottage gardening. At the back of this picture the tall, arching species rose, **Rosa glauca** (syn. *R. rubrifolia*), grows up to 4m/13ft. In front of it is **Rosa 'Sarah van Fleet'** a dense, thorny, scented shrub flowering recurrently all summer. **Rosa 'Fantin-Latour'** (in the foreground) grows as a large, spreading shrub (2m/6ft) with scented flowers in clusters, blooming in midsummer.

OLD VARIETIES OF ROSES survived in cottage gardens when the grand houses were landscaping with exotic trees and shrubs and creating large parks. Although rarely repeat-flowering, their scented flowers and leaves and soft hues will be reward enough for their space in the mixed border. Pruning can take the form of a light trim after flowering or a more severe clip in spring to improve their shape when their growth becomes lax. Other plants such as sweet peas can be grown through them to provide interest later in the summer.

Hardy geraniums such as pink *Geranium endressii* and blue *G. himalayense* are ideal ground-cover beneath roses.

Rosa **'Charles de Mills'** A gallica rose growing to an erect bush. Beautifully scented, flat and quartered flowers. Its petals can be dried to make pot pourri. ○, 1.5 × 1.5m/5 × 5ft

Rosa **'Complicata'** A hybrid between *Rosa gallica* and *Rosa canina* (Dog rose), it develops into a large shrub which can climb into a tree. It has large single flowers up to 12.5cm/5in in diameter. ○, ultimately to 3 × 3m/10 × 10ft

SHADE CLIMBERS

IN COTTAGE GARDENS WHERE SPACE WAS LIMITED, no habitat was left without plants. An old tree or shaded wall can be brightened by a shade-tolerant climber. Dark foliaged climbers can create an interesting 'gloomy' corner, or golden plants can provide light. The latter do particularly well in shade as they often scorch in sun, which is equally true of variegated plants. Finally, there are a few valuable roses which tolerate a degree of shade and still give a prolific display of blossom.

Rosa **'New Dawn'** Repeat-flowering and fragrant. May be grown as a climber or rambler. Subject to mildew if roots are dry. 6m/20ft

Rosa **'Madame Plantier'** Alba rose often grown as a climber. Strong-growing with lush green leaves. 2m/6ft

Rosa **'Félicité et Perpétue'** Clusters of small, double, blush, fragrant flowers in summer. 7m/23ft

◆ *Position by a sheltered wall for most profuse flowering.*

Lonicera tragophylla Best grown into a tree. Beautiful, but not scented, flowers in midsummer in terminal clusters. 9m/30ft

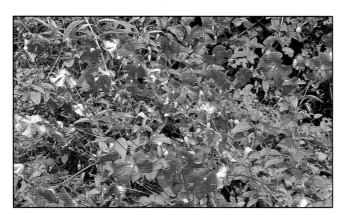

Hydrangea anomala ssp. **petiolaris** (**Climbing hydrangea**) Self-clinging and strong-growing with large corymbs of white flowers in summer. Ideal for a shady wall or to climb a tree. 15m/49ft

◆ *Can be grown as a shrub or trained over an old tree stump.*

Clematis viticella 'Abundance' Small crimson flowers produced freely in summer and early autumn. Ideal for growing into shrubs and trees. 3m/10ft

◆ *Prune by removing dead wood in spring rather than cutting down indiscriminately.*

SHADE CLIMBERS

Hedera helix 'Goldheart' Leaves with large yellow splash. This ivy is ideally planted on a north wall but will quickly reach the eaves of a house. 9m/30ft

When planted on house walls, ivies need to be pruned down to 60cm/2ft from the roof line each year.

Golden and variegated plants grow best in dappled shade to prevent scorching of leaves in full sun.

Soil can become very dry even in shade, especially under trees, so avoid planting moisture-loving plants here.

SUN LOVERS

WARM SUNNY CORNERS are ideal for many climbing plants, especially those which are a little tender. Trellises can be used to create this habitat in a sheltered part of the garden. Scented climbers release their aroma more readily in full sun. Care must be taken that the roots of plants such as clematis receive enough moisture when planted in full sun. It will save time if any climber which has a large appetite for water is well mulched in spring. This involves covering the earth around its feet.

Rosa **'Albertine'** A rambler and an old favourite despite some tendency to mildew. It produces only one display of flowers (midsummer) but is immensely floriferous during that time. 6m/20ft

Plants such as the passion flower which climb by tendrils are ideal for growing through roses on walls.

Clematis montana can quickly reach the roof of a house and clog drain pipes and lift roof tiles!

Plants which climb by twining around supports may 'strangle' plants they are growing with.

Rosa **'Rambling Rector'** Rampant hybrid rose forming a dense clump or growing up through a large tree. Small semi-double white flowers in corymbs with yellow anthers. Midsummer. 12m/40ft

Rosa **'American Pillar'** Small-flowered rambler with scentless deep pink flowers with white centre. Good for arches and pergolas. Midsummer. 5.5m/18ft

Clematis montana Rampant climber, flowering profusely in early summer. Flowers best in full sun. 6m/20ft+

***Vitis vinifera* 'Purpurea'** Black fruits and ornamental foliage. An attractive vine when trained in silver foliaged trees. 6m/20ft

Wisteria sinensis Fragrant flowers in slender racemes up to 25cm/8in long. Early summer. 12m/40ft

***Jasminum officinale* (Summer jasmine)** Semi-evergreen foliage and very fragrant white flowers. 4.5m/15ft

***Solanum crispum* 'Glasnevin'** Needs to be in sheltered position. Flowers are very fragrant. Summer/autumn. 6m/20ft

***Passiflora caerulea* (Passion flower)** Strong climber needing a sheltered position. Flowers borne singly on large stalks. Climbs by tendrils. 4.5m/15ft

Some climbers such as wisteria can be grown as standards by initial support of the central trunk.

Spend time concreting trellis and arches firmly in the ground. There's nothing sadder than a collapsed rose arch!

When planting rambler roses, clear a large area of turf around to ease the task of weeding at the base.

***Rosa* 'Paul's Himalayan Musk'** Rampant climber with sweetly scented flowers in hanging corymbs. Midsummer. 12m/40ft

***Parthenocissus quinquefolia* (Virginia creeper)** Rampant climber. Leaves are red in autumn but soon fall. 12m/39ft

SUMMER ONLY

***Ipomoea* (Morning glory)**
Heart-shaped leaves and twining stems with single open flowers in shades of blue, pink and lilac. Open in morning sun. Mid to late summer. ◯, 2m × 30cm/ 6 × 1ft

Wild vetches and vetchlings are attractive when allowed to grow up through other plants such as early-flowering shrubs.

Perennial sweet pea species such as *Lathyrus latifolius* can scramble over hedges and buildings but have no fragrance.

The old wood of ornamental brambles and raspberries dies back each year and flowers are formed on the new growth of the previous year, so prune with care in autumn.

SOME HERBACEOUS PLANTS exploit the hedgerow habitat to reach sunlight, including many members of the pea family. Herbaceous climbers can also be grown up established wall climbers, such as roses and honeysuckle, and sprawl over trees and shrubs in the border. Old-fashioned varieties of sweet peas grow well through shrub roses, their flowers always finding the sun.

Even some climbing vegetables, whether edible like runner beans or decorative like gourds, can be exploited attractively for their habits.

Climbing vegetables such as runner beans and climbing French beans grow well over arches covered with plastic mesh or netting. The beans are easily picked and make an attractive feature in a small garden. Sweet peas may be grown amongst them.

◆ *Simple plastic-coated arches are best for climbing vegetables and make for easy maintenance in winter.*

***Tropaeolum majus*
(Nasturtium)** Flowers throughout summer. Well-suited to pot growth. ◯, 2.4m × 45cm/8 × 1½ft

Tropaeolum speciosum Deep red flowers on climbing herbaceous stems. Ideal in evergreen hedge. Summer. 4.5m/15ft

***Lathyrus odoratus* (Sweet pea)** Scented flowers, pink, white, purple and lilac shades throughout summer in loose sprays. There are many named varieties and cultivars. Traditionally grown on hazel boughs lining the path to the cottage door, their sweet fragrance fills the air all around. Popular cut flower. The seeds of this hardy annual may be set in early spring but the plants are cut down by severe frosts. ○, 3m/10ft

***Lathyrus odoratus* 'Painted Lady'** This small-flowered deliciously scented variety has been in cultivation for centuries. Flowers two shades of pink.

3. COTTAGE GARDEN MAINSTAYS

There are plants which are so characteristic that one cannot imagine a cottage garden without them.

TALLER COTTAGE PLANTS

NOTHING EPITOMIZES A COTTAGE GARDEN MORE than the wealth of tall herbaceous plants that have been cultivated in them for hundreds of years. They were often grown so close together that no staking was necessary. Where land for growing food was scarce, the flower garden was often limited to a small strip next to the cottage or by the garden gate. Plants were swopped by neighbours and roots brought back by workers from the 'big house'. Wild flowers were introduced, especially those with double flowers or variegated leaves.

Dictamnus albus purpureus **(Burning bush)** This plant forms dense clumps with pink or white flowers in summer on long spikes. Aromatic leaves. 75 × 75cm/ 2½ × 2½ft

◆ *It prefers well-drained soil and light shade. On hot days, the oils produced by the leaves can be set alight.*

Geranium pratense '**Mrs Kendall Clark**' This form of meadow cranesbill grows into a large clump. Early summer. 1 × 1m/3 × 3ft

◆ *This will naturalize in open grassy places.*

Campanula persicifolia '**Telham Beauty**' An excellent border plant for sun or semi-shade. Summer. 1m × 45cm/3 × 1½ft

Lysimachia clethroides
forms a large clump in
moist soil, producing white
flowers in terminal curving
spikes. It is ideal for the
woodland border. Summer.
$1 \times 1m/3 \times 3ft$

Tall plants that rarely need staking
are valuable plants in the massed
planting of a border. Such a plant
is the pale yellow **Cephalaria
gigantea** growing up to 2m/6ft,
forming large clumps. Its flowers
are a valuable source of nectar. In
the foreground, **Campanula
latiloba** grows to 1m/3ft in sun or
semi-shade, forming dense mats.
Framing borders by clipped
hedges of box (*Buxus*) or *Lonicera
nitida* helps support taller plants.

TALLER COTTAGE PLANTS

Euphorbia amygdaloides var. **robbiae** Creeping underground rhizomes form dense patches. Best naturalized beneath shrubs. ◑, ●, E, 60 × 60cm/ 2 × 2ft +

Cutting back geraniums and campanulas after flowering may induce second flowering in late summer.

Plants with grey, downy foliage may be prone to mildew in damp conditions. Most thrive in warm, well-drained sites.

Lilies grown in pots and kept free of slugs can be used to fill gaps in borders after early summer flowering. Choose later-flowering, fragrant varieties.

Phlox 'White Admiral' One of the many scented forms of *P. paniculata*. Prefers slightly moist soil. Summer. 75 × 60cm/2½ × 2ft

Lychnis coronaria atrosanguinea A short-lived perennial preferring dry soils in full sun. Freely self-seeds. 60 × 45cm/2 × 1½ft

Asphodeline lutea (Yellow asphodel) Spikes densely covered with star-like flowers. Midsummer. 1m × 60cm/3 × 2ft

MIDSUMMER IN A COTTAGE GARDEN is a time of maximum growth. Plants associated with summer abundance begin to flower now, many providing valuable nectar for bees which ensure fertilisation in the kitchen garden. A mix of taller plants among lower growing flowers in cottage beds will emphasise the feeling of profusion.

Papaver orientale 'Charming' (Oriental poppy) Large crushed tissue flowers borne singly. 1 × 1m/3 × 3ft

Geranium sylvaticum 'Mayflower' This cultivar produces a mass of blue-purple flowers in late spring. 1m × 60cm/3 × 2ft

Alcea rosea (Hollyhock) Shades from dark maroon to pink and pale yellows. Late summer. 2m × 60cm/6 × 2ft

Anemone × hybrida (**Japanese anemone**) White, pink or rose flowers. Late summer/autumn.
1.2m × 60cm/4 × 2ft

Geranium psilostemon Large, free-flowering plant making excellent ground cover amongst shrub roses. Mid to late summer.
1 × 1m/3 × 3ft

Acanthus spinosus (**Bear's breeches**) Leaves deeply cut and spiny. Large spikes of flowers in mid to late summer. 1.2 × 1m/4 × 3ft

Lilium candidum (**Madonna lily**) Grows best in well-drained chalky soil, rich in humus. Midsummer.
1.2m × 30cm/4 × 1ft

Polemonium caeruleum album Self-seeding perennial. Flowers produced in early summer.
1.2m × 30cm/4 × 1ft

Polemonium reptans '**Lambrook Mauve**' Pale lilac-blue flowers in loose clusters. Early summer.
60 × 60cm/2 × 2ft

Iris germanica (**Bearded iris**) Various colours and forms. Early summer. ○, 1m × 60cm/3 × 2ft

◆ *Bearded irises and Oriental poppies complement each other perfectly.*

THE NATURAL STYLE OF COTTAGE GARDENS enables plants to die down in autumn without being cut back. Attractive seed heads provide form in the garden during the winter months.

Delphiniums Flowers from cream to blue and deep purple. Summer. 1.5m × 60cm/5 × 2ft

◆ *Cover crowns with grit in spring against slug attack.*

Campanula persicifolia
Drooping open bells. Blue, white and double forms including 'cup and saucer'. 75cm × 45cm/2½ × 1½ft

Campanula alliariifolia
Flower bells hang to one side of a tall stem in summer. Moist soil. ◑, 75cm × 45cm/2½ × 1½ft

***Nepeta × faassenii* (Cat-mint)** Sprays of lilac-blue flowers in midsummer. Aromatic foliage. 45 × 45cm/1½ × 1½ft

***Aconitum napellus* (Monkshood)** All parts are poisonous. Late summer. 1.2m × 45cm/4 × 1½ft

Achillea filipendula 'Gold Plate' Achilleas attract beneficial insects to the garden. Mid/late summer. ○, 1.2m × 60cm/4 × 2ft

Eryngium bourgatii Thistle-like heads in mid/late summer over deeply cut leaves. ○, 60 × 30cm/2 × 1ft

Campanula latiloba alba Spreads to large clump with pyramidal spikes and masses of open flowers. 60 × 60cm/2 × 2ft

◆ *This is an excellent plant to grow through shrub roses, as here.*

Paeonia lactiflora 'Bowl of Beauty' Scented flowers in which stamens are replaced by petal-like filaments. Grows to a large clump. Summer. 1 × 1m/3 × 3ft

Aster novi-belgii 'Fellowship' Spreads to large clump and rarely needs staking. Needs thinning by division every few years to prevent it getting 'woody'. Nectar plant. Late summer. ○, 1 × 1m/3 × 3ft

Penstemon 'Red Knight' Penstemons are wonderful long-flowering plants. Mid to late summer. E, 1m × 45cm/3 × 1½ft

Kniphofia 'Atlanta' Forms large clumps with red and cream inflorescence. Early summer. ○, E, 1m × 45cm/3 × 1½ft

Physalis alkekengi (Chinese lantern) Long cultivated for bright orange seed heads dried for winter decoration. 45 × 60cm/1½ × 2ft

SHADY PLACES

Anemone blanda Spring flowers up to 3cm/1½in. in diameter. Blue, mauve, pink and white forms. Naturalizes in grass beneath trees. 15 × 10cm/6 × 4in

Lysimachia punctata (Garden loosestrife) Large, spreading perennial. Will naturalize in moist places. Summer. 75 × 60cm/ 2½ × 2ft

Primula sieboldii alba Flowering stems with up to twenty flowers; frilled edges. Also pinkish-purple forms. 20 × 30cm/8in × 1ft

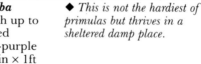

◆ *This is not the hardiest of primulas but thrives in a sheltered damp place.*

Symphytum 'Hidcote Blue' Excellent for naturalizing in damp woodlands or ditches. Flowers in spring. 60 × 60cm/23 × 2ft

Lamium maculatum roseum This deadnettle makes excellent ground cover. Pale pink flowers in spring. 30 × 60cm/1 × 2ft

Allium moly Summer flowers in terminal umbels. Naturalizes in well-drained semi-shade. 23 × 30cm/ 9in × 1ft

Primula elatior (Oxlip) Hybrid between *P. veris* (Cowslip) and *P. vulgaris* (Primrose), which naturalizes in shade. Late spring. 30 × 30cm/1 × 1ft

Geranium clarkei 'Kashmir White' Ideal for underplanting roses and light-shade shrubs. Summer. 45 × 45cm/ 1½ × 1½ft

DAPPLED SHADE will support a rich variety of herbaceous plants, many providing ground cover. A garden seat under an old tree is an ideal way to enjoy the garden on a hot summer's day. Golden and variegated plants prefer partial shade to prevent scorching.

Soil in shade may be damp or dry in midsummer. Check before planting up that a site damp in spring retains some moisture in high summer.

Dappled shade will support a wide range of flowers. Delicate, leafy plants will grow in parts of the garden not in direct sunlight.

Golden plants add interesting patches of light in partial shade and their yellow leaves are not scorched by strong sunlight.

Mertensia virginica (**Virginia cowslip**) The plant flowers in spring and is dormant by midsummer. 60 × 45cm/2 × 1½ft

Pulmonaria saccharata (**Lungwort**) Leaves are well-spotted and flowers blue and purple. Spring. 30 × 45cm/1 × 1½ft

Polygonatum × hybridum (**Solomon's seal**) Naturalizes in woods and old garden sites. Early summer. 1m × 30cm/3 × 1ft

Convallaria majalis (**Lily of the valley**) Forms spreading mats by rhizomes in woods and scrub. Several varieties are in cultivation including a pink form.

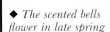
◆ *The scented bells flower in late spring*

GROW WILD

A SMALL MEADOW PATCH enhances any garden. Wild flowers can easily be introduced by putting well-established plants into the ground or by sowing seeds on bare earth. Best results are obtained if the plot is cut once or twice at about the same time each year. The cut herbage is left to dry so that seeds can fall to the ground, and is then removed. A nutrient-poor patch of ground is ideal for a wild flower garden, preventing grasses from dominating. Wild flowers are then able to spread freely.

Primula vulgaris (**Primrose**) Shady banks and woods. The pale simple flowers are one of the first signs of spring. 15 × 15cm/ 6 × 6in

Swathes of uncut grass by neat lawns can give a soft and dreamy feel to a cottage garden. Removal of unwanted plants and careful introduction of new ones can create an effect that pleases the eye.

Mown paths, leading to sitting areas in a 'wild meadow', provide viewing spaces to see both plants and the many insects in this habitat.

Geranium pratense (**Meadow cranesbill**) Flowers best in open site or sunny hedge-bank. Summer. 1m × 60cm/3 × 2ft

Scilla non-scripta (**Bluebell**) Fleshy linear leaves with central flower stems. Naturalizes in woods and hedgebanks. Very fragrant. Spring. 45 × 30cm/1½ × 1ft

◆ *Bluebells flower best in dappled sunlight rather than deep shade.*

Knautia arvensis (**Field scabious**) Growing in meadows and on dry banks, it flowers in midsummer. 45 × 30cm/1½ × 1ft

Pentaglottis sempervirens (**Alkanet**) Intense blue flowers mix well with *Silene dioica* (Red campion). Late spring. 70 × 30cm/2¼ × 1ft

Ornithogalum umbellatum (**Star of Bethlehem**) Forms a pyramidal raceme. Clump-forming. Spring. 45 × 30cm/1½ × 1ft

***Papaver rhoeas* (Field poppy)** Self-seeding in open ground, gravel and sparse grassland on a variety of soils. Summer. 60cm/2ft

***Campanula rotundifolia* (Harebell)** Hardy plant of sparse grassy places. Mid- to late-summer. 20 × 10cm/ 8 × 4in

***Silene dioica* (Red campion)** Self-seeding perennial. Late spring/early summer. 1m × 30cm/3 × 1ft

GROW WILD

When sowing a wild flower garden, sow different species in drifts of differing shapes and sizes. If sowing a mixture of herbs and grasses, sow thinly to avoid grasses dominating other seedlings.

***Cardamine pratensis* (Lady's smock)** Naturalizes in moist grassland. Pale lilac flowers. Also a double form. Spring. 30 × 20cm/1ft × 8in

***Filipendula ulmaria* (Meadowsweet)** Musky scent and 'frothy' cream flowers. Damp soil. Summer. 60cm/2ft

The rich diversity of life sustained by the tall herbage of wild flowers and grasses can be enhanced by the introduction of old garden varieties.

◆ *Clipping back vegetation in late summer allows for vegetative regeneration before winter sets in.*

SELF-SEEDERS

MUCH OF THE APPEAL OF AN INFORMAL BORDER is the chance appearance of self-sown plants. Freshly cultivated old cottage garden soil often throws up a variety of annuals such as poppies. A collection of annual seeds mixed in a bucket with little soil can be sown amongst perennials in a border. This random sowing gives a more natural effect than contrived sowing of single varieties in drifts.

The self-seeding of hardy annuals and biennials such as *Lunaria annua alba* (white honesty), *Meconopsis cambrica* (Welsh poppy) and *Myosotis* (forget-me-not) are reminiscent of the natural distribution of plants in the wild: dense patches, becoming sparser, as one species merges into another in drifts between perennial clumps and shrubs. Contrived sowing results in a tidier garden but may lose much of the charm of the so called 'untidy' garden.

Clarkia elegans White, purple, scarlet and salmon shades. Early summer. ○, 60 × 30cm/2 × 1ft

Iberis umbellata **(Candytuft)** A hardy annual with flowers of purple shades, in early summer. ○, 30 × 20cm/1ft × 8in

Lunaria annua **(Honesty)** A hardy biennial. Large, heart-shaped leaves and scented flowers. Late spring. 1m × 45cm/3 × 1½ft

Lunaria annua alba **(White honesty)** Seeding in sun or semi-shade, its pure white flowers are lovely in the evening. Late spring. 1m × 45cm/3 × 1½ft

◆ *Flat, paper-like seed pods dry on the stem and can be picked for winter decoration.*

SELF-SEEDERS

***Papaver somniferum*
(Peony-flowered poppy)** A
variable annual with single
or double forms from pale
lilac to deep pink petals
with frilled edges. Summer.
1m × 30cm/3 × 1ft

IF USING ANNUALS to create drifts of
colour, then single varieties can be
sown or transplanted in overlapping
areas. Careful weeding in spring helps
select self-sown annuals as they pop
up here and there.

Salvia sclarea turkestanica
A robust form of clary sage.
Well-drained, sunny place.
Midsummer. 1.2m × 60cm/
4 × 2ft

***Meconopsis cambrica*
(Welsh poppy)** Annual or
short-lived perennial. Early
summer 30 × 30cm/1 × 1ft

***Aquilegia vulgaris*
(Columbine)** Shades of
mauve, purple, pink and
white. Early summer.
1m × 45cm/3 × 1½ft

***Delphinium gracilis* (Rocket
larkspur)** Hardy annual
with long, loose racemes of
blue or violet flowers.
Flower spike can be dried.
Midsummer. 1m × 30cm/
3 × 1ft

***Hesperis matronalis* (Sweet
rocket)** Self-seeding, short-
lived perennial. Wonderful
fragrance. Early summer.
1.2m × 30cm/4 × 1ft

***Nigella damascena* (Love-
in-a-mist)** Flowers in shades
of blue, mauve, pink and
white. Summer. 60cm ×
23cm/2ft × 9in

***Myosotis sylvatica* (Forget-
me-not)** Biennial or short-
lived perennial. Open
ground or woodland.
Spring. 30 × 15cm/1ft × 6in

48

Calendula officinalis
(Marigold) Hardy annual.
Orange or yellow. Flowers
from spring to winter.
20cm/8in

Limnanthes douglasii
(Poached egg plant)
Annual. Open, sunny site
with cool roots. Summer.
15 × 10cm/6 × 4in

Eschscholzia californica
(Californian poppy)
Midsummer. ○,
30 × 15cm/1ft × 6in

◆ *Pick the long seed pods
just before they ripen and
dry in a warm place.*

Digitalis purpurea
(Foxglove) Short-lived.
White, pink or purple
forms. Early summer.
1.5m × 30cm/5 × 1ft

Oenothera biennis **(Evening
primrose)** Fragrant in the
evening. Self-seeding
biennial. Midsummer.
1.2m × 30cm/4 × 1ft

***Viola tricolor* 'Sorbet
Mixed'** Annual or short-
lived perennial. Damp,
shaded sites. Summer.
15 × 15cm/6 × 6in

◆ *This may gradually seed
back to wild species.*

Many annual species do not
like being transplanted.
Broadcast sowing into open
ground or in irregular-
shaped drills achieves the
best planting effects in a
cottage garden.

4. BY THE HOUSE

Even in a small garden you will want herbs and sweet-smelling plants close by the house.

CONTAINERS

Ivy-leaved *Pelargonium* **'Yale'**

ALMOST ANY PLANT can be grown in a container providing it is adequately fed and watered. Containers can be used to give height in borders and to provide interesting textures and focal points in the garden. They can be used to raise some plants, such as nasturtiums, above slug-height and tender plants can be moved out to summer borders. Some plants such as the old double primroses and lilies prefer to be freshly cultivated each year and are ideal pot subjects.

Old wheelbarrows make excellent containers for plants such as nasturtiums, courgettes or even potatoes. More decorative planting with geraniums and trailing pelargoniums helps brighten the summer garden.

◆ *Fill the base of the wheelbarrow with upturned turves to help with moisture retention and feeding.*

This witty little bird has been clipped out of box and sits on his nest against the wall.

Courgette (zucchini) grown in a pot within a decorative chimney pot. It will need to be kept well watered to crop.

Strawberries fruit from this jar, where they have been planted within the pouches.

◆ *Give this kind of jar an open position to enable the fruit to ripen on all sides.*

Where soil is poor or space needed for vegetable growing, a collection of tender plants in a variety of terracotta or earthenware pots adds interest and colour.

◆ *Large pot-grown exotics can be sunk in borders to fill in spaces later in the season.*

CONTAINERS

Sempervivums encrust the layers of this wall pot like jewels. A good choice as they are wonderfully decorative, need heat and tolerate drought. Choose those that form small rosettes for such a planting.

Container-grown plants will need regular feeding and watering so should not be too far from the house.

Container-growing is a chance to be adventurous and experimental with plantings. Many vegetables can be successfully grown in containers and interplanted with decorative plants.

SCENTED PLANTS

Rosa 'Président de Sèze'
One of the best gallica roses
for the garden, its large,
scented flowers are
produced for a single
period in midsummer. ○,
1.2 × 1.2m/4 × 4ft

**Clematis montana
'Tetrarose'** Bronze foliage
and lilac-rose flowers on a
lovely climber that grows in
any aspect, through large
trees or over out-houses.
Early summer. 9m/30ft

Syringa (Lilac) Flowers
should be removed as they
die. Lilacs prefer a rich,
lime soil and should be
regularly mulched. Early
summer. ○, 5 × 5m/
16 × 16ft

THE THERAPEUTIC EFFECTS OF SCENT have long been used in
gardens with plants such as lavender and rosemary planted
near back doors and along path edges. Few people can
resist running their hands over southernwood on a hot
summer's day. Night-scented plants such as *Hesperis
matronalis* (sweet rocket) were often planted near the house.
A mixed low hedge of aromatic herbs around the vegetable
plot will help to deter insect pests by masking scent.
Branches of aromatic plants such as southernwood can be
laid in bean and pea trenches to deter rodent pests.

Grow scented shrubs such as **lavenders**, scented **roses**, **southernwood** and **santolina** by a sunny seat. Aromatic plants produce volatile oils through the day, releasing them in sunshine and by touch. Scented flowers such as **pinks** produce their fragrance continuously. Pot-grown plants like *Lilium regale* and the tender *Acidanthera bicolor murielae* can be placed by seats when in flower.

HANDY HERBS

A traditional way of growing **parsley (Petroselinum crispum)** in a hanging basket. A large basket lined with moss and about twenty small parsley seedlings, provides fresh parsley for months.

Herbs are rarely showy plants but add soft colours, fragrance and attractive foliage to the flower border.

Resist the temptation to place your culinary herbs too far from the back door. Many herbs respond well to being grown in pots so can always be on hand.

Grow aromatic, heat-loving herbs between paving or gravel. The heat from these surfaces helps release aromatic oils in sunshine.

Mentha suaveolens **'Variegata' (Pineapple mint)** A decorative mint, but apple mint (*M. rotundifolia*) is preferable for its sweet spearmint flavour. ◑, 60 × 60cm/2 ×2ft

Bergamot, a rose, oregano and the little blue flowers of the annual self-seeding **borage,** (*Borago officinalis*).

Lavendula **(Lavender)** Hard prune or clip in late spring. Makes an excellent aromatic hedge. Varying heights. ○, E.

Thymus vulgaris **(Thyme)** Thymes may be clipped as a low, formal hedge or as an edging plant. ○, E, 30 × 30cm/1 × 1ft

Rosmarinus officinalis **(Rosemary)** Flowers early summer. Very aromatic. ○, E, 1.2 × 1.2m/4 × 4ft

Melissa officinalis **'Variegata' (Lemon balm)** Small, round leaves are lemon-flavoured. 60 × 60cm/2 × 2ft

Laurus nobilis **(Sweet bay)** withstands regular clipping and forms a good hedge in warmer areas. E, 3m/10ft

HERBS ARE AT THEIR BEST when grown in borders with other plants. Many herbs, such as mints, bergamot, lovage and sweet Cicely, prefer moist soil and do not thrive in the well-drained sunny places recommended for herbs such as sage and thyme.

Here a tiny patch of ground is used for growing a variety of vegetables, fruit and herbs.

◆ *The shaded areas beneath fruit bushes grow parsley and alpine strawberries. Mint grows in the hedge.*

***Allium schoenoprasum* (Chives)** Flowers and leaves used in cooking. Provides an attractive border or path-edge plant. 30cm/1ft

***Salvia officinalis* 'Purpurascens' (Red sage)** Aromatic leaves with blue flower spikes. Early summer. ○, E, 1 × 1m/3 × 3ft

Bronze fennel (*Foeniculum vulgare* 'Purpureum') with pink roses. Summer. 1.5m × 60cm/5 × 2ft.

◆ *The yellow flowers make good seed heads.*

5. SHRUBS AND TREES

These make a great impact in a small cottage garden, so must be chosen with care.

SMALL TREES *and* SHRUBS

Arbutus unedo (Strawberry tree) A bushy shrub or a small tree with glossy leaves. Very ornamental in autumn/winter when its white flower bells open at the same time as its 'strawberry' fruits that have matured from last year's flowers. E, 5 × 5m/16 × 16ft

Acer palmatum 'Dissectum'
Deeply lobed leaves turning yellow and red in autumn. Yellow flowers cluster in spring. Can be used as underplanting in moist, well-drained soil. ☽, 1.2 × 1.5m/4 × 5ft

Acer pseudoplatanus **'Brilliantissimum'**
Maples are a large genus with a wide range of leaf shapes and colours. They are often grown for their attractive autumn colours. 6 × 7m/20 × 23ft

WHERE SPACE IS LIMITED, careful selection of trees and shrubs is necessary, if only to avoid the 'murderous shrubbery' of Victorian times. If you plant shrubs and small trees in groups or add them to mixed borders, allow them unrestricted growth so that their natural shapes can be seen. Clearing around the base promotes growth but the roots should not be disturbed by digging. Climbing plants such as clematis and honeysuckle can be grown into trees and shrubs. Annual climbers like sweet peas can also be allowed to cling or twine over them, for a natural and profuse effect.

SMALL TREES *and* SHRUBS

Malus × purpurea Upright tree. Leaves flushed with purple. Profusely-flowering in spring with single deep cerise flowers 2.5cm/1ft diameter. Dull purple ovoid fruits. 7.5 × 5.5m/25 × 18ft

Crataegus laevigata **'Paul's Scarlet'** Deep cerise double flowers with musky fragrance in late spring. Slow-growing small tree which tolerates a wide range of soils and conditions. 6 × 5m/20 × 16ft

Robinia pseudoacacia **'Frisia' (False acacia)** Yellow leaflets in spring which turn greenish-yellow in summer, and fragrant cream flowers in pendulous racemes in spring. The bark is deeply furrowed and the twigs are spiny. The tree tolerates atmospheric pollution. 9 × 4m/30 × 13ft

◆ *The delicate foliage of robinias throws only light shade which means the tree can be underplanted.*

SMALL TREES *and* SHRUBS

THE LIMITED SPACE of the cottage garden means each plant must be 'good value' and provide a combination of attractive flowers and foliage, fragrance, fruit and good autumn colour. Those shrubs that are in flower for a long season are valuable, and so are those that bloom in winter or early spring.

Exochorda × macrantha **'The Bride'** Needs well-drained soil and a warm, sheltered spot. Early summer. 2.4 × 2.4m/8 × 8ft

Syringa vulgaris **(Lilac)** Lilacs are hardy shrubs or small trees with many species and hybrids, which tolerate most soils especially chalk. Their flowers in late spring have a delicious fragrance. 4 × 4m/13 × 13ft

The flutter and hum of butterflies and bees around the flowers of buddleja varieties in late summer is the reward for tolerating their rather uninspiring presence for the rest of the year!

Flowering shrubs such as deutzia and spiraea benefit from a pruning of their flower shoots when flowering has finished.

Philadelphus **'Sybille'** Spreading shrub flowering profusely in open sites. Fragrant flowers. Summer. 1.2 × 1.2m/4 × 4ft

Lupinus arboreus **(Tree lupin)** Spreading sub-shrub which is cut back by a hard winter. Light soils. Summer. 1 × 1m/3 × 3ft

Potentilla fruticosa Spreading shrubs of various flower colours. Some have glaucous foliage. Summer. 1.2 × 1m/4 × 3ft

Paeonia delavayi var. *ludlowii* Tree peony with single pale yellow flowers. Attractive palmate leaves, unusual seedpods and peeling orange bark. Early summer. Ultimately 2.4 × 2.4m/8 × 8ft

◆ *Tree peonies burst into life in spring, when old dead wood can be pruned out.*

Lavatera olbia **'Rosea'** with
Clematis **'Royal Velours'**
Fast-growing sub-shrub with
pink 'mallow' flowers mid to
late summer. Prune out
dead wood in spring.
○, 2 × 2m/6 × 6ft

◆ *The rich tones of some of the
darker flowered varieties of
clematis need careful placing to
be effective.*

Cotoneaster frigidus
'Cornubia' Arching
branches bearing dense
clusters of flowers along the
stems followed by scarlet
berries. Cotoneasters attract
birds and insects into the
garden. E, 7 × 7m/23 × 23ft

Kolkwitzia amabilis (**Beauty
bush**) Spreading shrub with
arched branches. Profusely-
flowering in full sun. Early
summer. 2.4 × 2.4m/8 × 8ft

Deutzia × *elegantissima*
'Rosealind' Fragrant
flowers. For all types of
fertile soil. Summer.
1.2 × 1.2m/4 × 4 ft

Buddleja davidii Flowers
are produced on new wood
so prune hard back in late
spring in a small garden. ○,
3 × 3m/10 × 10ft

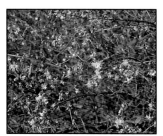

Lonicera fragrantissima
Large-spreading shrub.
Fragrant flowers in winter.
Semi-E in all but coldest
climes. 3 × 3m/10 × 10ft

Hamamelis mollis
Spreading shrub best grown
as standard. Acid, humus-
rich soil. Spring. 2.4 ×
2.4m/8 × 8ft

Buddleja weyerana **'Golden
Glow'** Large shrub for a
wild corner. Late summer.
○, 3 × 3m/10 × 10ft

SHADY CORNER

MANY FLOWERING SHRUBS AND TREES are shade-tolerant and may be used to provide colour and fragrance in a shady corner. Where mature trees already provide shade, underplant them with golden and variegated-leaved shrubs where they will not be sun-scorched. These can be underplanted with spring-flowering bulbs and shade-tolerant ground cover such as vincas (periwinkles) and hedera (ivies).

***Hypericum* 'Hidcote'**
Masses of flowers from mid to late summer. Hypericums thrive in a wide range of soils in sun or shade. E or semi-E, 1.5 × 1.5m/5 × 5ft

In a small cottage garden, underplant trees with fragrant, flowering shrubs and put herbaceous ground cover under those shrubs to utilize every niche.

Golden and variegated-leaved shrubs can be planted in shade to give splashes of light and draw the eye towards a focal point such as an arch or seat.

When planting groups of shrubs together, remember that foliage and form are more lasting than blossom or fruit. Plant contrasting textures and shapes.

Corylopsis sinensis (syn. *C. wilmottiae*) Delicate shrub or small tree with yellow flowers in spring. 4 × 4m/ 13 × 13ft

◆ *The flowers which hang in dense racemes are deliciously scented.*

Cornus kousa Shrub or small tree, not for chalk soils. Summer. 6 × 5m/ 20 × 15ft

***Philadelphus coronarius* 'Aureus'** Hardy shrub with clusters of cream flowers. Golden foliage. 1.5 × 1.2m/ 5 × 4ft

Hardy fuchsias are invaluable for colour in summer/autumn. Delay pruning until spring.

Neillia thibetica Suckering shrub with arching stems. Ideal in mixed border or wild garden. Summer.
2 × 2m/6 × 6ft

◆ *Neillia is especially attractive when grown in a mixed hedge underplanted with geraniums and campanulas.*

The lacecap hydrangeas flowering summer/autumn have particularly graceful flower-heads. This example is 'Blue Wave'.

Clematis armandii A rampant climber when grown in sheltered semi-shade. It has creamy flowers in late spring and glossy leaves. Prune after flowering. E, 6m/20ft+

***Camellia japonica* 'Nobilissima'** Peony-form flowers in early spring. Camellias need a slightly acid or neutral soil.
3 × 2m/10 × 6ft

◆ *Camellias may need some protection in exposed, cold regions.*

SPACE-SAVING FRUIT

SOME VARIETIES OF SOFT FRUIT, such as raspberries, will tolerate dappled shade. If these fruit bushes are underplanted with alpine strawberries, any awkward shaded corner can become productive. Climbing soft fruit like *Rubus* species (blackberry, bramble, etc.) may also be grown over mature hedges, and pruned down to ground level in the winter.

The warmth and shelter of old walls are ideal for espalier fruit trees such as cherry and pear. Espalier and cordon-grown fruit trees or bushes can be used as living trellises to separate gardens into smaller areas. Rhubarb and marrow will grow on old compost heaps.

Pears generally flower earlier than apples and respond well to being grown in the shelter of an old wall as an espalier. Prune in frost-free winter weather. If planting more than one, allow 6m/20ft between half-standards and 7m/23ft between standards.

For many centuries decorative ways of growing fruit trees have been devised. These methods, such as training large shrubs as standards or growing them as cordons and espaliers, are very useful in a small garden where they enable a greater variety of fruit to be included. Here two varieties of apple are growing on low, 'step-over' cordons, and staked, standard gooseberries are underplanted with strawberries.

FRUIT FEASTS

OLD-FASHIONED ORCHARDS with their rich varieties of fruit are becoming a thing of the past. Growing old varieties will help to preserve them and, although cropping may be lighter, the flavour and texture may be superior to modern varieties. Some varieties of apple, such as 'Discovery', crop heavily even on a small tree. Dwarf rootstocks enable most gardens to grow several fruit trees.

Alpine strawberries are accommodating enough to be tucked into odd corners and will tolerate shade.

Spring flowers can be grown under the spreading shade of an apple tree. Plant primulas and narcissi or marrows and rhubarb.

◆ *Remember when planting under fruit trees that you will need to pick the fruit or collect windfalls.*

Blackberry produces a prolific amount of fruit in late summer. Many cultivated varieties. Up to 2m/6ft

Mespilus germanica
(**Medlar**) Small, attractive
spreading tree. Pear-like
fruit. 4 × 4m/13 × 13ft

Currants May be grown as
bushes or standards or
trained against wall or fence
as cordons. Fruit
midsummer. 1.2m/4ft

The hardy gooseberry can be grown as a
broad bush in a hedge or trained as a
small standard. Fruit early summer.
1.2 × 1.2m/4 × 4ft

◆ *The flavour of gooseberries develops
well in cool growing conditions. There
are dessert or culinary varieties.*

6. WATER

*A water feature, no matter how small,
can bring a garden to life.*

POOLS WILD *and* FORMAL

Nymphaea **(Water lily)** An aquatic plant whose floating leaves and flowers provide valuable shade for aquatic life. Stout rhizomes spread quickly in pools and still water.

When starting a new pool allow time for oxygenating plants to become established before introducing larger aquatic plants.

Drainage from pools into marshy areas extends the rich planting sustained by moist habitats. A gravel or stone area around the pool prevents grass species from 'clogging' the pool-edge.

If pools are not fed by natural water, underground pipes can take storm water from the house guttering to the pool.

NO HABITAT IS MORE PLEASING than pools and bogs. Plants quickly become established with lush growth and wildlife such as dragonflies and amphibians soon appear. A garden seat near the pool is a must as is a fence if young children are around. Small formal pools, edged with slabs or stone, with clear water can reflect a shrub or border as well as grow more choice aquatic plants.

Camassia leichtlinii Blue or creamy flowers on long, attractive spikes in late spring. 1m × 30cm/3 × 1ft

Trollius chinensis **'Golden Queen'** Plant of moist, shady meadows. There are other paler forms. Early summer. 60 × 30cm/2 × 1ft

Geum rivale **'Leonard's Variety'** Water avens tolerate any good garden soil. Early summer. 45 × 45cm/1½ × 1½ft

FORMAL POOL

Planting is restrained to enable shape and reflective qualities of water in the pool to be enhanced. One or two choice species may be added to the water feature.

◆ *Many formal pools have fountains; the therapeutic sound of running water adds to the tranquillity of a garden.*

GRASS EDGES OF WILD POOLS create a cool, humid area around the pond. Informality of outline is helped by planting ornamental grasses, sedges and bamboos, or you may surround it with a bog garden in which you can grow moisture-loving plants you cannot place elsewhere.

Caltha palustris **(Kingcup)** Strong, clump-forming marsh plant. Also white and double forms. 45 × 45cm/1½ × 1½ft

INFORMAL POOL

Planting can include plants such as *Mentha aquatica* (water mint), *Lychnis flos-cuculi* (ragged robin), *Iris pseudacorus* (yellow flag) and aquatic plants such as *Ranunculus lingua* (greater spearwort). Different plants will dominate from year to year.

Plants quickly become established and naturalized in a bog-garden. **Carex pendula** (Drooping sedge) forms a large clump (1.5m/5ft). **Primula japonica** has candelabra whorls of flowers on spikes, (75cm/2½ft) and freely self-seeds. **Iris sibirica** (opposite) grows into a large clump in damp soils in a range of wonderful colours, flowering in early summer. Selective removal of some plants in the bog garden prevents them becoming too dominant.

NEVER DRAIN DAMP AREAS in the garden! They are difficult to create artificially and support a wide variety of attractive plants. These quickly spread or seed down, so weeding is minimal. Stepping stones or raised paths will provide easy access, and underground hoses are useful for very dry seasons. If you do not already have a boggy area, it is worthwhile creating one adjacent to a pond or in a low-lying part of the garden.

Astilbe × *arendsii* **'Erica'** This graceful astilbe forms a large clump in partial shade or sun, but it must have moisture for its roots. It flowers from mid to late summer. 1 × 1m/3 × 3ft

BOGGY BITS

Filipendula rubra large, robust plant with frothy terminal flower heads of deep pink in summer. Forms large clumps in moist soil. 2m/6ft

The foliage of ferns and sedges provides form and interest in boggy areas and helps screen other flowering plants which become dormant in late summer.

Aromatic shrubs such as *Myrica gale* (bog myrtle) will survive in acid boggy conditions and release a wonderful aroma. *Populus balsamifera* (balsam poplar) grows to a large tree with heavy balsam scent.

Willows tolerate moist soils and many varieties have wonderful bark and flower buds for winter and early spring interest.

ARTIFICIAL BOGS CAN BE CREATED by hollowing areas to a depth of about 45cm/1½ft and lining them with polythene. Cover the lining with about 15cm/6in of gravel and replace the topsoil in the pit. Try to prevent moisture evaporating by covering the soil with mulch before dry periods occur.

Thalictrum aquilegiifolium A strong-growing perennial with attractive foliage. Masses of tiny 'frothy' flowers mauve to white. Summer. 1.2m × 60cm/ 4 × 2ft

Primula japonica '**Postford White**' A lovely candelabra primula for semi-shade, flowering in early summer. 45 × 45cm/1½ × 1½ft

Athyrium filix-femina (**Lady fern**) Prefers slightly acid soil. Double-pinnate fronds give it graceful form. ◑, 1 × 1m/3 × 3ft

Primula florindae Flowers in a single panicle, yellow or reddish amber-orange. Broad leaves. Summer. ◑, 1m × 60cm/3 × 2ft

Primula pulverulenta Candelabra whorls of up to twenty flowers in shades of red to white. Summer. To 1 m × 45cm/3 × 1½ft

Chaerophyllum hirsutum **'Roseum'** Delicate umbels in late spring, growing from rosette of leaves. 60 × 60cm/2 × 2ft

Ligularia przewalskii Leaves with irregularly cut margins. Numerous flowers in summer. ◑, 1.5m × 60cm/5 × 2ft

Lobelia **'Dark Crusader'** Flowering in late summer/autumn, one of several richly coloured hybrids. ○, 75 × 75cm/ 2½ × 2½ft

Leucojum aestivum (**Summer snowflake**) Bell-like flowers. Sun or semi-shade. Summer. 60 × 20cm/ 2ft × 8in

Epilobium angustifolium album (**White rosebay willow herb**) Not as invasive as true form. Summer. 1.2m × 60cm/ 4 × 2ft+

Iris kaempferi (**Japanese flag**) This large-flowered beardless iris is also obtainable in white, pink and mauve forms. Summer. 75 × 75cm/2½ × 2½ft